AN
ALBUM OF
THE JEWS
IN
AMERICA

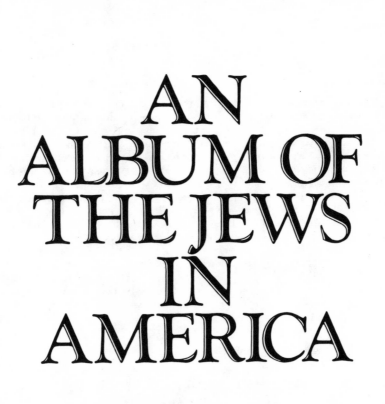

AN ALBUM OF THE JEWS IN AMERICA

YURI SUHL

William Loren Katz
Consulting Editor

Franklin Watts, Inc.
New York 1972

Photographs courtesy of:

AMERICAN JEWISH ARCHIVES: pages 8(top), 13(inset), 20(top right and bottom), 25, 27, 35, 36, 39, 68(bottom). THE BETTMANN ARCHIVE: opp. second half-title, pages 5(bottom), 8(bottom), 58(top). BROWN BROTHERS: pages 2, 43, 47(center), 51, 71. THE CANADIAN PRESS: page 85. CBS TELEVISION NETWORK: page 78(right). CINEMABILIA: page 84(bottom). COLUMBIA RECORDS: page 81(top). CULVER PICTURES: pages 63(bottom), 67(right). HEBREW UNION COLLEGE–JEWISH INSTITUTE OF RELIGION: page 74. JOHN HOPF: pages 13, 14. LEVI STRAUSS & CO.: pages 30, 32. LIBRARY OF CONGRESS: page 78(left). MUSEUM OF THE CITY OF NEW YORK: pages 10, 20(top left), 54, 64(top right and bottom), 79. *Frontispiece:* Photograph by Berenice Abbott for Federal Art Project "Changing New York". *Cover, Pages 44(top), 47(bottom):* Photographs by Byron, The Byron Collection. *Pages 45, 47(top):* Photographs by Jacob A. Riis, The Jacob A. Riis Collection. NATIONAL FOUNDATION FOR INFANTILE PARALYSIS: page 86(bottom). NEW YORK PUBLIC LIBRARY PICTURE COLLECTION: page 5(top.) OREGON HISTORICAL SOCIETY: pages 29, 40, 60(top). UNITED PRESS INTERNATIONAL: pages 58(bottom), 80, 81(bottom), 82(right), 83, 84(top), 86(top). UNITED STATES DEPARTMENT OF THE INTERIOR: pages 67(left), 68(top). WIDE WORLD: page 82(left). YIVO INSTITUTE FOR JEWISH RESEARCH: pages 44(bottom), 48, 60(bottom), 63(top). THE ZIONIST ARCHIVES AND LIBRARY: page 57.

Cover design by Toni Goldmark
Photo research by Wesley Day

Library of Congress Cataloging in Publication Data

Suhl, Yuri, 1908-
    An album of the Jews in America.

    (Picture albums)
    SUMMARY: Discusses the contributions of Jewish immigrants to the history and culture of the United States from 1492 to the present.

    1. Jews in the United States–Pictorial works.
2. Jews in the United States–Juvenile literature. [1. Jews in the United States] I. Title.
E184.J5S88   301.45′19′24073   72-5475
ISBN 0-531-01513-0.

Contents

AN ALBUM OF THE JEWS IN AMERICA

Dinner at Ellis Island, where most immigrants entered the United States.

1

The Jews Seek a New World

Americans sometimes forget that it was the immigrants who came here from various lands, and their sons and daughters after them, who made this country what it is today. Some were lured to these shores by the promise of opportunities for business and personal fortune that a virgin land holds out to the newcomer. But many who came to the New World were people in search of freedom and security denied them in the Old World. The Jews were such a people, a people in search of a home and a haven. They cherished the freedoms they found here, and together with other immigrants they struggled to enlarge these freedoms and protect them, sometimes at the cost of their lives, until America became a hope for all who sought a refuge from tyranny and oppression.

It could be said that the story of the Jews in America begins with Columbus's journey to America. Some historians believe that the first European to set foot on the soil of the new land was a Jew named Louis de Torres, one of six Jews in Columbus's crew of ninety. But Jews did more than accompany Columbus on his westward voyage; they played a leading role in making that voyage possible.

Columbus had strong and influential Jewish allies in the royal court of Spain. They were Louis de Santangel, chancellor of the royal household, Gabriel Sanches, chief treasurer of Aragon, and Cuan Cabrero, the king's chamberlain. It was they who finally convinced King Ferdinand and Queen Isabella of the importance of Columbus's expedition. And Santangel personally lent the court 17,000 florins to pay for outfitting the three vessels.

Jews also helped provide Columbus with the tools for navigation, for they were among the best mapmakers and astronomers of Portugal and Spain. The most famous of them was Abraham Ben Samuel Zacuto, who was attached to the Spanish court. It was his astronomical tables that guided Columbus through the uncharted seas.

(3)

That was in 1492, a milestone year in human history. But for the 300,000 Jews of Spain 1492 was a sad and tragic time, for it was in that year that King Ferdinand and Queen Isabella presented them with the most difficult choice: to renounce their religion and adopt the Christian faith, or to leave their country within four months. Most Spanish Jews chose exile rather than conversion.

From 1492 on, there were, officially, no Jews in Spain, only Marranos—Jews who had submitted to baptism but who secretly practiced Judaism. These Marranos lived in constant danger of being discovered by the Inquisition set up by the church to ferret out converted Jews suspected of clinging to Judaism. They were tortured to confess this sin, and some were burned at the stake.

And so on the very day that Columbus and his three vessels sailed from the small port of Palos, the port of Cadiz was crowded with Jewish refugees setting out on a long journey of exile. They searched for a new home.

The majority fled to nearby Portugal where the king allowed them to stay a limited time. But in 1496 the new king issued a decree that was only too familiar to Jews: baptism or expulsion. Now Portugal, too, had Marranos and an Inquisition.

It was natural for Jews to cast a hopeful eye westward, in the direction of the new lands opened up by Columbus and the explorers who followed in his trail. That was why Jews were found among the very early settlers in south, central, and north Americas.

The New World benefited greatly from the skills and experiences these newcomers brought from the Old World. But the peace and security the Marranos had hoped to find in their new home did not last very long. The Spanish and Portuguese Inquisitions they fled from soon followed them all the way to South America. Once again Marranos suspected of practicing Judaism in secret were tortured and burned at the stake.

Soon Marranos flocked to Recife, Brazil, to enjoy freedom under Dutch rule. As Protestants under Spanish rule for many years, the Dutch had also had a taste of the Spanish Inquisition. As a result they were sympathetic toward other victims of religious persecution.

A large number of Jews came from Holland to Recife, bringing with them a rabbi and a cantor. They traded with Holland and other European countries, built homes and a synagogue, which they called Kahal Kodesh, and thus formed the first Jewish community in the New World.

Intolerance toward Jews did not begin with the Spanish Inquisition of 1492. Hundreds of years earlier, Jews in Europe were stoned (left) and massacred. Below, The grand council of the Inquisition determined the fate of people brought before it. Anyone who confessed to practicing Judaism faced possible death.

But the life of peace and security for the Jews of Recife was short-lived. In the continuous wars between Holland and Portugal, Holland suffered a major defeat when the Portuguese recaptured Recife in 1654. The Jews fought valiantly on the side of their Dutch ally who was unable to stem the Portuguese tide. Once again they took the road of exile, the majority going to Holland. Those who chose to remain in the New World fled to other colonies under Dutch rule. New Amsterdam, which later became New York, was one of these.

2

A New Home in New Amsterdam

One September day in 1654, twenty-three Jewish refugees from Recife sailed into the harbor of New Amsterdam. After a long and stormy journey on the French frigate, Saint Catherine, they were happy to touch land again. Not just any land, but Dutch-ruled land where they expected to be welcome and enjoy the same freedoms Jews were known to enjoy under the Dutch. One can imagine, therefore, the shocked surprise of these tired refugees when Peter Stuyvesant, the governor of the colony, asked them to leave. But they refused to budge.

As far as Peter Stuyvesant was concerned, the landing of the refugees was only temporary. He immediately sent a letter to the Dutch West India Company in Holland, asking for permission to oust them from New Amsterdam. That company had appointed him governor of the colony. He spoke of the Jews as a "deceitful race" and urged that they "be not allowed further to infect and trouble this new colony."

But the directors of the Dutch West India Company thought otherwise. In their reply to Stuyvesant in April, 1655, they not only granted the Jews permission to remain in the colony but also granted them the right to "travel and trade." They reminded Stuyvesant that Jews were among the important investors in the Dutch West India Company.

Unhappy with the Company's decision, Stuyvesant dispatched another letter to Holland in October 1655, citing another reason for withdrawing liberty from the Jews. "Giving them liberty," he wrote, "we cannot refuse the Lutherans and Papists [Catholics]." He might as well have added the Quakers, the Presbyterians, and the Mennonites, who were also part of the New Amsterdam community. For Peter Stuyvesant there existed only one religion: the Dutch Reformed Church. Anyone who practiced another faith was regarded with suspicion and hostility.

The Jews also sent letters to Amsterdam and, with the support of

influential Jews in the Dutch West India Company, they won the right to trade, own real estate, and build homes for themselves. They were refused permission to build their own synagogue. So their freedom of worship was restricted to the privacy of their homes.

There were other rights, however, that could be won. The right to guard the colony under arms was one of them. Peter Stuyvesant denied the Jews that right and insisted that they pay a guard exemption tax instead. Their spokesman, Asser Levy, refused to pay and insisted on standing guard like any other burgher. He won his case. The right of citizenship was also denied. Once again Asser Levy challenged Peter Stuyvesant's denial of the "small burgher right" to Jews and won. A victory for the Jews turned into a victory for the other inhabitants of New Amsterdam who were discriminated against by Peter Stuyvesant. This was particularly true in the struggle for freedom of religion. Later, when New Amsterdam came under English rule and was called New York, the small Jewish community held on to its hard-won freedom, and in some areas of civil rights enlarged them. In 1730, they finally established a synagogue, called Sheareth Israel—Remnant of Israel.

A Swedish traveler passing through New York later wrote that the Jews there "possess great privileges. They have a synagogue and houses . . . and are allowed to keep shops in town. They have, likewise, several ships which they freight and send out with their goods; in fine, the Jews enjoy all the privileges in common to the other inhabitants of this town and province."

The traveler's claim that the Jews "enjoyed all the privileges in common to the other inhabitants" was exaggerated. They could not, for instance, participate in the election of members to the General Assembly, and they were denied the right to act as witnesses in a court. And when the Swedish traveler spoke about the ships some sent out with their goods he must have had in mind men like Lewis Gomez, a Marrano born in Spain who, with his family, escaped to New York, where he was able to practice Judaism openly. In time Gomez became the leading merchant of New York as well as a leader of the Jewish com-

Peter Stuyvesant (above) the governor of New Amsterdam in 1654, when Jews first arrived in that colony. Stuyvesant tried but failed to have the Jews removed. Below, New Amsterdam as it appeared in 1656, two years after the first Jews arrived there.

(9)

munity. One of his five sons lived to fight in the American Revolution. Gomez conducted trade with other colonies in the New World and with various countries in the Old World as well. Frequently his ships returning from abroad would bring not only merchandise but also Marranos from Spain, Portugal, or South America. And like other merchants, Jewish, Protestant, and Catholic, Gomez also engaged in the very profitable slave trade that was flourishing in the colonies.

But not all Jews were merchants and traders. Most of them earned their living as craftsmen and artisans. There were shoemakers and silversmiths, candlemakers and house painters, bakers and tailors, tobacconists and wigmakers.

Above, the Sheareth Israel graveyard still stands in New York City. It was the cemetery for early members of the first synagogue in America. Below, Moses Levy and his wife, Grace Mears Levy, were among the prosperous Jews in New Amsterdam in the late seventeenth and early eighteenth centuries.

3

Rhode Island:
Separation of Church and State

The only other colony on the eastern seaboard where Jews were welcome was the colony of Rhode Island. It was founded by Roger Williams, a strong believer in the separation of church and state. He also believed that all peoples, including Jews, should enjoy freedom of worship. Thanks to Williams's enlightened leadership Rhode Island became the first colony in North America that was free from religious persecution.

The first Jewish settlers in Rhode Island came from as far away as Holland and Poland, from the West Indies and nearby New Amsterdam, and of course Marranos from Portugal and Spain were happy to find a place where they could practice their Judaism openly. Like the Marrano Gomez from Spain, the Marrano Aaron Lopez from Portugal also escaped to the New World with his family. He settled in the seacoast town of Newport, R.I., and became the major shipping merchant on the eastern seaboard. At one time he had as many as thirty vessels carrying his merchandise around the world and to the coastal cities of the colonies at home.

Few Newport Jews were as wealthy as Aaron Lopez. The majority were either small tradesmen or workers and so when the time came to

Right, a copy of the petition filed in 1762 by Aaron Lopez and Isaac Elizar in Newport requesting permission to become naturalized citizens of the colony of Rhode Island. Inset, Aaron Lopez, a wealthy Jewish merchant, came to Rhode Island from Portugal.

To the honble Superior Court of Judicature
held at Newport in & for the county of Newport
the first Tuesday of March a d 1762.

Aaron Lopez and Isaac Elizar, Persons professing
the Jewish Religion between the Hours of nine & twelve
in the Forenoon being present in said Court do give
the said court to understand & be informed that they
were born out of the Liegeance of his Majesty the King
of Great Britain but have resided in the Colony of
Rhode Island upwards of seven Years without being
Absent at any one Time two Months, And therefore
they pray that they may have Leave to take the Oaths
of Allegiance &c and to conform themselves to the
Directions of an Act of Parliament of the 13.th Year
of his late Majesty George the Second entitled an
Act for naturalizing such foreign Protestant's &c
as are settled or shall settle in any of his Majes-
=tys Colonys of America, And as in duty bound
they will ever pray &c

Aaron Lopez
Isaac Elizar

build their synagogue they had to appeal to other Jewish communities for help. Jews in all parts of the world responded. In 1763 the Jews of Newport celebrated the dedication of the second synagogue in North America, which they named Yeshuat Israel—Salvation of Israel. Today, Yeshuat Israel, the Touro synagogue of Newport, is the oldest synagogue in the United States. In 1946 it was declared a national historic site.

Interior and exterior views of the Touro Synagogue of Newport, Rhode Island. It is the oldest synagogue in the United States and is now a national landmark.

4

Jews in America's Colonies

There were no synagogues in any of the other colonies for the simple reason that there had not been enough Jews in any of them to form a stable Jewish community. The few here and there were made to feel like outsiders. The Puritans of New England expressed great admiration for the Jewish Bible and respect for the Hebrew language but as for the Jews themselves, they shared Peter Stuyvesant's prejudices and did not welcome them in their midst.

There were few Jews in Pennsylvania, Maryland, Virginia, or South Carolina. In 1775, on the eve of the American Revolution, there were about 1,000 Jews in all the colonies. The general population of non-Jews totaled over 2.5 million.

The economy in the colonial days was mainly agricultural, and most people lived on farms. For the non-Jewish population it was their natural way of life, so they continued to do in the New World what they had always done in the Old World. But in the Old World Jews had usually been forbidden to own land. In any case, their lives were too uncertain to be saddled with ownership of immovable property. These circumstances compelled them to live in towns and cities where their chief occupations were as artisans, craftsmen, and merchants. It was therefore natural for them to continue their way of life in the New World. The thriving candle industry in Newport is a good example of how skills acquired in the Old World could become the basis for a useful and prosperous enterprise in the New World. In the colonial days, when candles and oil lamps were the chief means of lighting the homes and the streets, it was one of the women's many chores to make their own candles. The process they employed was a long and time-consuming one. Some of the Marrano refugees from Portugal knew a better way of making candles than the slow and painstaking method of collecting bits of tallow and melting them on the wicks. They knew how to make candles and oil from whale sperm. Not only was the process quicker, but the product was superior. At one time there were close to twenty factories in Newport busy making whale sperm candles and whale sperm lamp oil, which were widely used not only in the colonies but were also exported to other countries.

By the second half of the eighteenth century there were also Jewish communities in Philadelphia and Charleston and smaller groups in Virginia, Georgia, and in other colonies. But only in New York and Newport were there synagogues. Annexed to the synagogues were the first Hebrew schools in North America where Jewish children were taught not only Hebrew and the Bible but also Spanish, English, writing, and arithmetic.

The inhabitants of the several Jewish communities scattered among the colonies were certainly more prosperous than were most of the Jews in the Old World. But they were still a long way from enjoying full religious freedom and political equality. Only in New York were Jews allowed to participate in the election of legislators: enlightened Rhode Island, which granted them full religious freedom, denied them the right to vote. In some colonies they were not even welcome as residents, and in some their religion was barely tolerated.

5

Revolution:
Freedom and Equality for All

It took a revolution to bring about a fundamental change in the concept of freedom and equality for all. The American Revolution of 1776 ushered in a new era in the life of the colonies. And the small Jewish community played an honorable role in this turning point of American history.

The first Jew to fall in battle in America's War of Independence was Francis Salvador, whose early ancestry could be traced back to the Portuguese Marranos. The following two lines engraved on his tombstone in South Carolina eloquently express the spirit of the many Jewish patriots in the struggle for America's independence:

> *True to his ancient faith, he gave his life*
> *For new hopes of human liberty and understanding.*

When the British captured Savannah in 1778, they hauled Mordecai Sheftall, a Jew born in Georgia, off to a prison ship. Sheftall was the head of the revolutionary committee of Georgia and a member of the Georgia Brigade, in charge of arms and food supply. The British knew they had caught a "very great rebel," and ordered him kept under special guard. But they were never able to make Sheftall tell them where the Americans kept their supplies, and the prisoner finally escaped to Philadelphia. At the end of the war this patriot was awarded a grant of land for his outstanding contribution to America's War of Independence.

Benjamin Nones, a French-born Jew, enlisted in the continental army as a private and rose to the rank of major and staff officer. His famous commander, General Pulaski, cited him for "the bravery and courage which a military man is expected to show for the liberties of his country . . ."

When the government was in desperate need of money to carry on the war, Jewish businessmen played their part in financing the Revolution. Some, like Isaac Moses of Philadelphia, and Jacob Hart, Sr., of Baltimore, made personal loans to the government. Others supplied the army with uniforms and blankets, with rifles and gunpowder. Those who owned ships turned them into raiding vessels to fight the enemy on the high seas, ran an armed blockade against British merchandise, and sank British vessels.

The man who did more than any other single individual in obtaining urgently needed funds for the government to carry on the war of Independence was Haym Salomon, an immigrant from Poland. Salomon landed in New York in 1772. He joined the Sons of Liberty, an organization of patriots who supported the Revolution. When the British captured New York, Salomon was arrested as a spy. Once freed, he helped French and American prisoners of war to escape. He even convinced Hessian mercenaries to desert the British ranks. When the British were about to arrest him again, Salomon fled to Philadelphia.

Though he arrived in that city penniless, he quickly resumed the brokerage business that he had started in New York. Before very long he was deeply involved in raising money for the revolutionary forces. It is estimated that Haym Salomon raised $200,000 to help finance the revolution. He became known as the "Broker to the Office of Finance" of the United States.

Not all colonials sided with the rebels. Among the Jews, too, there was a conflict of loyalties. This burning issue divided families and congregations. Some were Tories, who wanted the colonies to remain under English rule. David Franks, the eldest of the prominent Franks family of Philadelphia, remained a Tory throughout the war, but the cousins, Isaac and David Salisbury Franks, both served as high-ranking officers in the continental forces.

When it became clear that Washington would temporarily have to abandon New York, Rabbi Gershom Mendez Seixas, an ardent patriot for the revolutionary cause, urged his congregation to leave the city with him. To remain, he argued, would amount to giving support to the British. Not all heeded the rabbi's advice. Some of the wealthier members, who feared that the revolution might deprive them of their wealth, sided with the British. But the majority of the congregation followed their rabbi. This was in 1776. Not until 1783, when the continental

forces drove the British out of New York, could they end their self-imposed exile and return to their homes.

After the war was over, the colonies, having won their independence from Britain, settled down to build in peace and to enjoy the freedoms for which they had fought. In the belief that one of the basic freedoms in a true democracy is freedom of religion, the complete separation of church and state, the founding fathers wrote Article VI into the federal Constitution in 1787. The article says: "No religious test shall ever be required as a qualification to any office or public trust under the United States." Two years later Article VI was further strengthened by the first amendment to the Constitution, which states: "Congress shall make no law respecting an establishment of religion, or prohibiting the exercise thereof." This was a new and revolutionary concept in those days when every land had its official religion, supported by the state, and all other religions were either persecuted or merely tolerated.

To the Jewish community which, by the end of the war had grown to six congregations, this declaration of religious freedom had a special meaning. It had been the hope of finding this freedom that brought them to these shores. Now, thanks to the victory that they had helped to win, their dream of full freedom had become the law of the land.

Above left, Isaac Moses of Philadelphia helped the cause of the American Revolution by lending money to the government. Above right, the most famous and perhaps most important Jew at the time of the Revolution was Haym Salomon, a Polish immigrant who became known as the "Broker to the Office of Finance" of the United States. Cousins David Franks (below left) and Isaac Franks were both high-ranking officers in the continental forces. The portrait of Isaac Franks was painted by Gilbert Stuart, the famous American artist who is probably best known for his paintings of George Washington.

(21)

6

Upholding the Constitution

Most of the thirteen states ratified (approved) the Constitution by 1788. But there were exceptions. On the question of religious freedom not every state was ready to surrender old beliefs or part with old prejudices.

In Maryland, by state law, no citizen of that state could hold public office unless he made "a declaration in a belief in the Christian religion." This automatically deprived the Jews in Maryland of their legal and political rights. Nearly ten years after the drafting of the federal Constitution, the Jews of Maryland still had to petition the state legislature to remove this restrictive provision from the state constitution. They lost. It was not until 1826 that full religious freedom became the law of the state. The long and bitter fight was led by legislator Thomas Kennedy, a Christian and an immigrant from Scotland. He pointed out that there were very few Jews in Maryland, ". . . but even if there were only one, to that one we ought to do justice. . . ."

The longest struggle for full religious freedom was waged in North Carolina. The constitution of that state prohibited the holding of public office by anyone who denied "the being of God or the truth of the Protestant religion. . . ." This provision affected atheists, Catholics, and Jews alike. It was not until 1868 that North Carolina joined the other states in granting full religious liberty to its citizens.

7

A New Democratic Spirit

There were signs everywhere of a new democratic spirit abroad in the land. When Congregation Mickveh Israel of Philadelphia made a public appeal for funds to meet its debts, among the first to respond was Benjamin Franklin. And in New York, the steeple on Trinity Church was built partly with financial assistance from Jews. In Rhode Island, Brown University opened its doors to Jewish students, and in New York, Rabbi Gershom Seixas was invited to serve as a trustee of Columbia College. The Jews of Newport engaged a Christian architect to draw up the plans for their synagogue. The Gold and Silversmiths' Society of New York elected a Jew, Myer Myers, as its president.

The liberal atmosphere generated by the victorious revolution and the adoption of the Constitution and the Bill of Rights now made it possible for Jews to participate actively in the social, civic, and political life of the country. Organizations such as the humane societies, the General Society of Mechanics and Tradesmen, the Masons, the Sons of St. Tammany and the Jeffersonian Democratic and Republican Societies all included Jews in their memberships.

American Jews wrote to friends and relatives in the Old World, telling them of the freedom and equality they were enjoying. Even the Chinese Jews in far off Kaifung read about it in a Hebrew letter written by two New York Jews: "We in America, in New York and in other Places, live in great security. Jews together with Gentiles sit in judgment on civil and criminal cases. . . ."

8

A New Wave of Immigration

The American union was growing by leaps and bounds. The thirteen colonies that existed at the time of the Revolution had, by 1812, grown to twenty-four states. And the number of Jews had increased from 1,000 in 1776 to 6,000 in 1826.

This sharp rise in the Jewish population was due to a new wave of immigration that resulted from the social and political upheavals in Europe at that time. The French Revolution with its slogan of liberty, equality, fraternity, and the subsequent Napoleonic wars, had toppled the old feudalistic regimes. It had ushered in a period of enlightenment in central Europe that was marked by a spirit of freedom and democracy. The Jews were liberated from the ghettos and, for the first time in centuries, enjoyed certain political and economic rights.

But with Napoleon's defeat at Waterloo in 1812, the old feudalistic monarchs returned to power. And oppression of the people was once again the order of the day. Particularly hard hit were the Jews. The ghetto walls were rebuilt and a wave of anti-Semitism surged through Europe. In parts of Germany, anti-Semitism took the form of pogroms, in which Jews were murdered, their homes and businesses burned.

As a result, Jews, along with other oppressed and economically deprived peoples of Europe, emigrated to America in large numbers. And America, growing and expanding, was glad to have them. The Jewish immigrants who came here during the first half of the nineteenth century were markedly different from those of the earlier colonial period. The difference was one of cultural and historical background. The early Jewish settlers in North America were mostly refugees from the Spanish and Portuguese Inquisitions—Sephardic Jews whose mother tongue was Spanish or Portuguese. The immigrants of the later period were Ashkenazim, Jews from central and eastern Europe, mainly from Germany.

By the time this second wave of Jewish immigrants arrived, some of the earlier settlers had already achieved prominent positions in the economic, social, political, and cultural life in the country.

An outstanding Jewish figure in nineteenth-century America was Mordecai Manuel Noah (1785–1851), whose father fought in the American Revolution. Philadelphia-born, Noah moved to New York, where he became prominent in both literary and political circles. In addition to being a popular playwright and leader of the Jewish community, he held such varied positions as surveyor of the Port of New York, sheriff of New York County, and judge of the New York Court of Sessions. In 1813, President James Madison appointed him United States consul to Tunis. He planned, unsuccessfully, to resettle Jews persecuted in Europe, particularly in Germany, into a "new Jewish state" in America.

9

The War of 1812

When the United States went to war with Britain in 1812, Jews once again rallied to the defense of their country. In addition to the many privates in the armed forces, there were the officers: Mordecai Myers and Aaron Levy from New York; Joshua Moses from Pennsylvania; Myer Moses from South Carolina; Abraham A. Massias from Georgia; Judah Touro from New Orleans; and Benjamin Nones, a veteran of the Revolutionary War.

The outstanding Jewish officer in the War of 1812 was navy captain Uriah Phillips Levy. When Levy was given command of a ship, he banned flogging on his ship. His refusal to flog men was considered so dangerous that efforts were made to remove him from command. He knew those arrayed against him were also motivated by anti-Semitism, and the secretary of the navy came to his defense by pointing out that "the strong prejudice against him" was largely due to Levy "being of the Jewish persuasion." Levy proudly asserted his pride in being Jewish and stepped up his campaign against flogging. Finally, in 1862 Congress outlawed the flogging of seamen.

Above left, Judah Touro, son of Rabbi Isaac Touro of Newport, Rhode Island. Judah Touro earned a reputation on his own in his adopted city of New Orleans, Louisiana. He founded the first Jewish congregation there. Touro also is remembered for his bravery in the Battle of New Orleans when he was wounded in action, fighting the British under General Andrew Jackson. A wealthy shipping merchant and a generous philanthropist, he helped finance Bunker Hill Monument in Boston. Above right, Uriah Phillips Levy, the outstanding Jewish officer of the War of 1812, rose to the highest naval rank of commodore. Because of Levy, flogging was outlawed in the United States Navy. Below, Benjamin Nones, veteran of the Revolutionary War, once again donned his military uniform in the War of 1812.

(27)

10

Immigrants from Germany

Between 1820 and 1850, as a result of a steady stream of European immigrants, the population of the United States increased tremendously. Germans made up the majority of these immigrants, among them thousands of Jews. In addition to the hunger and political tyranny that motivated the large German immigration, Jews had reasons of their own for leaving Germany. They were pinned under the heavy burden of anti-Jewish laws and various taxes aimed specifically at them.

America, eager for new labor power, beckoned to these immigrants. It offered them economic opportunities and the political freedoms denied them by their homelands.

The defeat of the revolution of 1848, which swept through Austria-Hungary and the German states, gave further impetus to German immigration. Thousands fled in the wake of new repressive measures instituted by the ruling monarchs. Many refugees were Jews. By 1850 the number of Jews in the United States had risen to 50,000, and the number of Jewish congregations to 77.

Most of the Jewish immigrants from Germany settled in cities where there were already sizable Jewish communities, such as New York, Philadelphia, Baltimore, Boston, Cincinnati, and New Orleans. Others followed the trail of the non-Jewish German immigrants who went West to do what they had done in their homelands—till the soil. And some, who for centuries had been denied the right to own land and lacked the experience in farming, came as itinerant peddlers.

Bernard Goldsmith (left), who served as mayor of Portland, Oregon, in 1869 and 1870, was a Jewish immigrant who planted his roots beyond the crowded cities of the Eastern seaboard. Right, Portland's Jewish community built this synagogue in 1888.

(28)

Average Daily
1902 Circulation
For 7 Months—
Jan., Feb., Mar., Apr., May, June, July, Aug.
Guaranteed **49,223**

The B

VOLUME XCIII.   47th Year.   SAN FRANCISCO, SATURDAY

LEVI STRAUSS, MERCHANT AND PHILANTHROPIST, PASSES AWAY

Was Called by Death While He Lay Asleep.

Sudden Attack of Heart Disease the Cause.

Levi Strauss, the well known merchant, banker and philanthropist, died suddenly last night at his residence on Post and Leavenworth streets. Mr. Strauss had been indisposed for several days past, having suffered a slight attack of heart failure, but it was not believed that he was seriously ill, and the announcement of his death came as a shock to his friends and business associates.

At 9 o'clock last night Mr. Strauss seemed in better health than at any time during the past few days. His spirits were good and he laughed and chatted with members of his household during the evening. Shortly after 9 o'clock he retired and about midnight when the nurse went to his room he was found dead on the bed, death having evidently come while he slept.

Levi Strauss was one of the most prominent Jewish citizens of this city. Born in Bavaria seventy-three years ago he came to San Francisco in 1854 and engaged in mercantile pursuits, accumulating a large fortune. He was the founder of the Levi Strauss Company, and at the time of his death was the president of this corporation. He was also a director of the Nevada Bank of this city and the Liverpool, London and Globe Insurance Company.

Mr. Strauss was rated several times a millionaire, and he gave his wealth with a generous hand. He was a member of several charitable organizations, and during his lifetime established twenty-eight scholarships at the University of California, which are known as the Levi Strauss scholarships.

Mr. Strauss was unmarried and was the last surviving member of his family.

The arrangements for the funeral have not been completed.

BAD WEATHER IN JAPAN CONTINUES

Levi Strauss.
(Taber, Photo.)

SOUSA CELEBRATES TENTH ANNIVERSARY

In the Decade He Has Given 4500 Concerts.

CHICAGO, Sept. 27.—The tenth anniversary of the formation of the famous organization, "Sousa and his Band," was celebrated here last night when "The March King" appeared be-

immense quantity of cable and other repair material which will be kept at the repair station. A plan is now being considered by the Department of Public Works whereby a plot of Government land in every way suitable for the purpose, but now under lease to the Inter Island Steam Navigation Company, may be leased to the cable company for a repair station, the Inter-Island Company being given another piece of land in another location, but suitable for their purposes in exchange.

SOUTH ... TO CH...

When Franklin ... his Southern ... fellow townsmen ... tion at the ... tions are now ... enthusiastic gatherings ... Iroquois candidate ... date from the ... theater. There ... greet his host ... the present plans ... addresses, one by ... other by former Gov ... Lane's campaign ... strongholds south ... unexpected weakness ... section. Everywhere ... ed by great crowds ... publicans have given ... ance of their support ... have taken heart ... and all of the Scott ... that Lane will get ... vote. Harrison G... that non-union men ... geles Times, and ... Governor Gage ... anything to do ... grown alarmed ... day morning he m... Lane, calling him ... jecting vigorously ... ing as man to man ... workingmen. This ... ened Lane material ... lieved that he will ... and that the best ... do is to get a sens...

11

Making a Living

The craftsmen among the immigrants—the tailors, shoemakers, tin-smiths, glaziers, goldsmiths, and cabinetmakers—could rely on their old crafts and trades and quickly adjust to their new homeland. But for those who had been merchants, peddling seemed a practical solution to the urgent problem of making a living. With a pack on his back that contained household wares, drygoods, and other necessities—merchandise he most likely had acquired on credit—the peddler would set out for the hinterlands. There he found customers who spoke his language.

At that time the horse and wagon was the sole means of land transportation and the farms and villages were long distances away from the towns and cities. So the peddler, who brought the badly needed goods into the customer's home, was a welcome visitor. And with the goods he carried news and gossip from the outside world to the isolated areas. Thus the peddler fulfilled a useful social and economic function during those pioneering days.

After saving a little money the peddler might buy a horse and wagon and free himself from the burden of the pack. Or he might take a liking to a village, open a retail store and settle there, watching the village grow into a town and expanding his business to keep pace with the growing population. With such early, modest beginnings, immigrant peddlers laid the foundations for some of the country's leading depart-

Not all Jewish merchants were peddlers. Levi Strauss, merchant, banker, and philanthropist, was a prominent citizen of San Francisco. Strauss, a German immigrant, created a mercantile empire that still thrives. "Levi's" is one of the most popular brand names known in the world. This is the account of Strauss's death in 1902 that appeared in a San Francisco newspaper.

(31)

ment stores, such as Macy's and Abraham and Strauss, both in New York City.

During the depression year of 1837 and after, efforts were made by groups of German-Jewish immigrants to settle on land and devote themselves to farming. And several Jewish farming colonies did spring up in different parts of the country. But with limited funds, no farming experience, and little support from the rest of the Jewish community these efforts soon failed.

An advertisement for products of Levi Strauss and Co., founded by the German immigrant of that name.

(33)

12

Religious and Cultural Reform

The influx of German-Jewish immigrants during the first half of the nineteenth century brought with it some radical changes in the structure of the Jewish community. As the Ashkenazim became the dominant force in the congregation they instituted reforms of both a secular and religious nature. Under Sephardic leadership Jewish life had been organized around the synagogue, but the Ashkenazim freed the philanthropic organizations, mutual aid societies, and fraternal orders from synagogue control. The New Israelite Sick-Benefit Society, founded in New York in 1841, stated in its constitution that "Our society should be independent of the synagogue." It was German Jews who in 1843 organized the Independent Order B'nai B'rith in New York. Today it is the largest Jewish fraternal order in the United States.

And there were also changes inside the synagogue. In some, English prayers were introduced to harmonize the services with the democratic spirit of the new homeland, and women no longer had to sit apart from the men on a curtained-off balcony. They could now share the same pew with their husbands. These practices were part of a movement called Reform Judaism, which had originated in Germany. The foremost leader of Reform Judaism at that time was Rabbi Isaac Mayer Wise (1819–1900), who arrived from Germany in 1846. When Rabbi Wise moved to Cincinnati in 1854 that city became the center of Reform Judaism.

The vestry room of Cincinnati's Mound Street Temple, which was demolished in 1961. It is believed that this is the room where the first class of Hebrew Union College met in October, 1875.

(34)

Michael, Rebecca, and Barnard Gratz, members of a family famous during the eighteenth and nineteenth centuries as merchants and civic leaders, were active in Jewish life.

13

Social Reform and Civil War

American Jews had shown little enthusiasm for the Mexican war of 1846–1848. Only a very few enlisted. In a letter that Rebecca Gratz wrote to a relative at the time, she said: "I feel so much more sorrow and disgust, than heroism in this war. When we were obliged to fight for our liberty, and rights, there was motive and glory in the strife, but to invade a country and slaughter its inhabitants, to fight for boundary or political supremacy is altogether against my principles and feelings." Evidently it was also against the principles and feelings of a large part of the Jewish community.

Jews also were aware of injustices dealt other minorities in America. They knew that freedom in America did not apply to everyone. It did not apply to the hundreds of thousands of black people who were slaves. The freedoms proclaimed by the Bill of Rights that "all men are created equal" and that they have "inalienable Rights to Life, Liberty and the pursuit of happiness," did not apply to them, nor to the Indians, nor to the women of the country. Jews were among those who sought to gain freedom and humane treatment for the poor, the sick, the helpless, the enslaved.

An outstanding Jewish woman of her time was the beautiful and wealthy Rebecca Gratz of Philadelphia (1781–1869). She devoted her life to aiding the poor and the orphaned and to improving religious education for Jewish children. In 1819, when the country had an economic depresion, she founded the Philadelphia Orphan Asylum and she is credited with establishing the first Jewish Sunday school in America. It is believed that she served as the model for the heroine Rebecca in Scott's novel, "Ivanhoe."

One of the leading social reformers in nineteenth-century America was Ernestine L. Rose (1810–1892), daughter of a Polish rabbi. She and her husband, William Rose, came to the United States in 1836. That same year she initiated a petition campaign for a bill to grant married women the right to own property. She was soon joined by other women. Her effort grew into a major petition campaign, which, after a twelve-year struggle, finally saw the passage of New York State's Married Woman's Property Act in 1848. It was the first legal victory for women's rights in that state and it sparked the beginning of a national women's rights movement.

Ernestine Rose was a frequent and forceful speaker at antislavery rallies and also an advocate of an improved public school system. Her eloquence earned her the title "Queen of the Platform." Although she was active outside the Jewish community, she never abandoned her Jewish identity and referred to herself as "a daughter of poor, crushed Poland, and the down-trodden and persecuted people called the Jews, 'a child of Israel'."

The question of slavery became America's most burning issue. The steady industrial growth of the North, based on a system of wage labor, could not be reconciled with the slave system that existed in the South. In addition there was the moral question. By the end of 1850, the abolitionist movement had become a vital force in the country, arousing thousands of people to the moral outrage of slavery. The Jewish community became as involved as the rest of the country.

Rabbi David Einhorn (1809–1879), a leader of Reform Judaism, and who, in the slave state of Maryland, preached fiery abolitionist sermons, stands out among Jewish abolitionists. So does August Bondi (1833–1907), another militant abolitionist and an Austrian immigrant,

Above, Ernestine Rose, an outstanding social reformer of the nineteenth century. Abolitionist William Lloyd Garrison considered her "one of the most remarkable women of the age." Below left, Dr. David Einhorn, a rabbi known for his antislavery sermons, was forced to flee Baltimore, Maryland, when a proslavery mob threatened his life. Dr. Einhorn escaped to Philadelphia and continued his fight against slavery. Below right, Polish-born scholar and linguist Michael Heilprin (1823–1888) was a Jewish abolitionist who brought to America a revolutionary background from the Old Country. Heilprin took part in the Hungarian revolution of 1848 under Kossuth. When the revolution was put down he fled to France. He landed in New York in 1856.

(38)

like Einhorn. Bondi and two other Jews fought beside Captain John Brown to keep the territory of Kansas free from slavery.

Another fighter for democracy who had to flee from his native Austria as a result of the counterrevolution of 1848 was Isidor Bush (1822–1898). He arrived in New York in 1849 and became the publisher and editor of the Jewish weekly, *Israel's Herald*. He later moved to St. Louis, where he was an active abolitionist and a prominent leader in the Jewish community.

As the antislavery sentiment in the country grew, the southern planters threatened to secede from the Union rather than abolish slavery. The same attitude prevailed among the Jewish plantation owners in the South, home to about 15 percent of the country's Jewish population. In the North, too, the business groups whose economic interests were closely tied to the production of cotton in the South were pro-slavery. Even the Bible was drawn into the conflict when the slave owners and their supporters argued that God was on the side of slavery.

The leading Jewish spokesman for the proslavery forces in the South was Judah P. Benjamin, a plantation owner and a senator from Louisiana. He had defended slavery in the Senate prior to the Civil War, and during the war he held the posts of secretary of war and secretary of state under Confederate President Jefferson Davis. He was considered the most brilliant member of the Confederate cabinet.

In April 1861, rebellious southerners captured Fort Sumter. This act sparked the Civil War. Most Jews in the North and the West, like the majority of the total population in these areas, rallied around President Lincoln in defense of the Union. Thousands of Jews joined the Union forces, and many distinguished themselves in battle. Seven received the Congressional Medal of Honor, the country's highest military decoration.

In other ways, too, Jews supported the Union cause, raising money for the soldiers and their families, knitting socks and sewing bandages, opening the Jews' Hospital in New York to the wounded, and joining the Red Cross of that time, which was called the Sanitary Commission.

During and after the Civil War, Jews continued to settle in the West. Beth Israel Synagogue, built in Portland in the 1860's, looks somewhat like a New England church.

14

The Big Wave

Beginning in 1880 there was a dramatic increase in the number of Jewish immigrants arriving in this country. This was the start of the third and largest wave of Jewish immigration. Jews from eastern Europe, particularly from Russia, were streaming into the United States at the rate of about 100,000 a year. As a result, the number of Jews in in this country rose from 300,000 in 1878 to 3,000,000 in 1914. This steady stream of Jewish immigration continued until 1924. Then, the passage of restrictive immigration laws all but clanged shut the door to the country.

The immediate causes of this mass migration of eastern European Jews were the brutal pogroms of 1879 and 1881 in Russia and Russian-held Poland. These were large-scale massacres, inspired by an anti-Semitic Russian government. They continued in following years and hung as a permanent threat over the largest Jewish community in Europe. Actually this was the czar's way of diverting the peasants' attention from the true source of their miserable existence. By putting the blame on the Jews, the czar could continue to take advantage of the poor and uneducated people he ruled.

Like their Sephardic brethren who had escaped from the Spanish and Portuguese Inquisitions, and their German brethren who had fled from the persecution of the Prussian monarchies, the Jews of eastern Europe found a home and a haven in the United States.

Although the majority settled in New York, many remained in other port cities, such as Boston and Philadelphia. Some went to Rochester, others as far west as Chicago. But wherever they went, their first contact was usually with HIAS, the Hebrew Immigrant Aid Society. Earlier immigrants had founded the organization in 1881 to give the newcomers a helping hand. HIAS was at the landing to assist with immigration problems; to help locate friends and relatives; to find a place to live; and, in some instances, even to find an immigrant that first job.

These immigrants at Ellis Island were part of the "big wave" that begin in 1880.

While poor immigrants were struggling to survive, there were earlier arrivals who were already prospering in America. This photograph shows a wedding dinner of a Jewish couple taken around 1910.

Below left, the inside of an immigrant's home in the early 1890's. Above, ready for the Sabbath eve in a coal cellar, early in the 1890's. Below, Hester Street, on New York's Lower East Side, around the turn of the century.

Invariably the immigrant's first home in New York was in a crowded tenement house on the Lower East Side. There rent was cheap and the neighbors were immigrants as well. And that first job was usually in some branch of the needle trades. By 1880 the manufacture of ready-to-wear clothing had become a booming industry in the United States. This business was largely in the hands of German Jews. The growing demand for mass-produced apparel created the need for a large labor force. The Jewish immigrants from eastern Europe filled that need.

Factory owners took advantage of the constant stream of laborers coming off the boats and they dictated working conditions. Wages were kept low—between three and eight dollars a week. And the work-day was long—between fourteen and sixteen hours. Factories were crowded, unsanitary, poorly ventilated, and hazardous. The immigrants called the factories "sweatshops." The following lines are from the poem, "The Sweatshop," by the Yiddish labor poet, Morris Rosenfeld, who was himself a needle-trades worker:

> So wild is the roar of machines in the sweatshop
> I often forget I'm alive in that din . . .
> The clock in the shop, even he toils forever . . .
> I feel that his pendulum lashes me, prods me,
> to work ever faster, to do more and more.

These sweatshop conditions continued into the twentieth century. They made tuberculosis a common disease among needle-trades workers. And they led to such tragedies as the Triangle Shirtwaist Fire of 1911, which occurred in a New York sweatshop and took the lives of 143 young women, most of them Jewish. "Drape yourself in black, you Golden Land!" cried out the poet Morris Rosenfeld. "Too deep your crime, too horrible your shame."

Some immigrants who had been craftsmen in the Old Country, such as carpenters, glaziers, house painters, cigar makers, and jewelry makers, were able to avoid the sweatshop by making a living at their old skills. Others managed to open a grocery or candy store, to become

Above, a twelve-year-old boy is among the workers in this sweatshop, about 1889. Center, the charred remains of the sweatshop where 143 women died in the tragic Triangle Shirtwaist Fire of 1911. Below, street vendors on Hester Street, 1898. Pushcarts were a common sight well into the twentieth century.

a pushcart peddler in the Jewish neighborhood, or to peddle drygoods from door to door.

Still others turned their backs on the sweatshops, the crowded tenements, and the cities, and set out to become in their new homeland what their old homeland had never let them be—tillers of the soil. They were a group of young immigrants who called themselves *Am Olam* (Eternal People). Aided by the HIAS, by the Jewish Alliance founded in 1891 for that purpose, and by the wealthy Jewish philanthropist Baron de Hirsh, these "back-to-the-soilers" and their followers established agricultural colonies in various parts of the country from New Jersey to North Dakota. With few exceptions their existence was short-lived. They failed for the same reasons as the immigrants of an earlier period—lack of agricultural experience and insufficient funds. Still, the urge on the part of some Jews to live on the land persisted long into the twentieth century.

For most of the Jews who arrived in the 1880's the pressures of everyday life did not afford such experimentation. Unskilled, penniless, and faced with the immediate problem of providing for themselves and their families, they had to resort to the needle trades, which required no prior experience.

Above and left center, part of the Jewish farming colony of Carmel, New Jersey, as it appeared in 1889. Right center, Aaron Barony and his family were among the Jews who formed an agricultural colony in North Dakota late in the 1880's. Below, a banquet held in 1915 by the Federation of Jewish Farmers of America.

(49)

15

The Jewish Labor Movement

The workers struck back at the inhuman sweatshop conditions by organizing themselves into labor unions. Because they were Yiddish-speaking they found it necessary to form their own unions. But at the same time they were part of the general American labor movement and participated in its struggles for better working conditions. The United Hebrew Trades of Greater New York and Vicinity, founded in 1888, gave rise to a number of other unions, not all of which were limited to the needle trades.

Two of the most powerful and influential unions to emerge from the early Jewish unions were the International Ladies Garment Workers Union (ILGWU), organized in 1900, and the Amalgamated Clothing Workers Union, in 1914. In the first two years of its existence the ILGWU carried out 189 local strikes and won 158.

The greatest militancy and membership growth for Jewish labor unions took place between 1907 and 1914. During those years about 200,000 workers, led by Jewish unions, were involved in strikes that embraced a number of cities from New York to Chicago. The manufacturers frequently responded to these bitter struggles for higher wages, shorter hours, and union recognition by resorting to police brutality and by causing the arrest of hundreds of workers. It seemed as if nothing could stop their effort to break the strikers' spirit and thwart the growth of their unions. But quite the opposite happened. The United Hebrew Trades, which had a membership of 65,000 in 1910, had, by 1914, reached 750,000.

Above, Samuel Gompers, one of America's outstanding labor leaders, speaking at a strike meeting at Cooper Union, in New York City, in 1908. Below, union members of different nationalities and religions unite to demand an eight-hour workday.

Typical of the militant mood that prevailed among the sweatshop workers in those days was the general strike of the 20,000 ladies' shirt-waist-makers, which became known as the "Uprising of the 20,000." The strike, led by a young waistmaker, Clara Lemlich of Local 25 of the ILGWU, lasted from July 1909 to February 1910. All efforts on the part of management to break the strike, including the arrest of 723 workers, failed. The strikers' victory—shorter hours, higher wages, and union recognition—was an inspiration to other unions and was cheered by the entire American labor movement.

Other women who played leading roles in the Jewish labor movement in those years were Rose Schneiderman of the United Hat and Cap Makers Union, and Bessie Abramowitz of the United Garment Workers of America.

Encouraged by the waistmakers' recent victory, more than 50,000 cloakmakers went out on strike in July 1910. This strike, which was the biggest in New York and which dragged on for two months, is known as "The Great Revolt." Though the workers' victory was only partial, it had great effect on American labor. It introduced into the labor movement the concepts of collective bargaining and compulsory arbitration. The settlement was negotiated by Louis D. Brandeis, the "People's Lawyer." In 1916 he was appointed a justice of the United States Supreme Court.

The Jewish labor unions that came into being as a result of the mass immigration from eastern Europe generally favored socialism over capitalism. They were led by militant Socialists who labored in a struggle against capitalism for the benefit of *all* workers.

This concept of unionism was at variance with that of the American Federation of Labor, organized in 1886 and led by Samuel Gompers, a Jewish immigrant from England. Gompers believed in unionism "pure and simple" and was against using the labor union as a base for social reform. He favored capitalism over socialism.

With the passage of time the Jewish labor unions abandoned their Socialist orientation. Though the leadership continued to be Jewish, the membership began to change as a result of the restrictive immigration laws of 1922 and 1924. Other ethnic and minority groups, such as Poles, Italians, blacks, and Puerto Ricans, entered the needle trades in increasing numbers. By 1950 the membership of the Amalgamated and the ILGWU was only about one-fourth Jewish.

These Jewish unions were the first to conceive the plan of auxiliary, or fringe, benefits for their members. They introduced unemployment insurance long before the government did. Their benefits grew to include medical services, low rental housing projects, cultural programs, and summer camps. The pioneering of the Jewish labor unions in the expansion of benefits for their members served as a model to other unions. It also benefited the entire American labor movement.

The two best-known Jewish labor leaders, Sidney Hillman (1887–1946) of the Amalgamated, and David Dubinsky (1892–   ) of the ILGWU, made their impact on the American scene beyond their roles as union leaders. During World War II, Hillman was appointed by President Franklin D. Roosevelt to serve as director of the labor section of the War Production Board. Dubinsky was a founder of the American Labor party in New York and later of the Liberal party.

16

Fraternal Organizations

Even before they built their labor unions the Jewish immigrants banded together in mutual aid societies called *Landsmanshaften*. The members of a *Landsmanshaft* were people from the same town or region in the Old Country. In addition to sick benefits and interest-free loans, these societies gave the newcomers a sense of ease and security that comes from being among one's own townsmen.

With the growth of the Jewish labor movement came the need for a Jewish fraternal order based on the principle of self-help rather than charity. The Workmen's Circle (Arbeiter Ring), founded in 1900, filled that need. Like the Jewish labor movement as a whole, it was Socialist oriented. It also conducted a lively cultural and educational program.

In 1933 a disagreement within the ranks of the Workmen's Circle led to the formation of the left-wing Jewish People's Fraternal Order. The Zionist wing in Jewish labor, which in 1905 organized the Jewish Socialist Labor party — Poale Zion — had its own fraternal organization, the Jewish National Workers Alliance.

In the meantime, the German fraternal order, B'nai B'rith, had shifted its emphasis from self-help to large-scale philanthropy and an active concern for the civil and political rights of Jews at home and overseas. With its Anti-Defamation League, the B'nai B'rith developed into the most important defense organization of the American Jewish community.

J. G. Phelps Stokes campaigning on the Socialist ticket in 1908 among the immigrants on the Lower East Side of New York.

17

Zionism

As a result of the Russian pogroms in the 1880's Jewish nationalist groups called "Love of Zion" sprang up in eastern Europe. Their aim was to go to Palestine, where they would pioneer in the establishment of Jewish farming settlements. These scattered groups combined into one organization named BILU, which in Hebrew stands for "House of Jacob, come and let us go."

Some BILU groups actually did go to Palestine but most of them came to the United States. Here the "Love of Zion" societies, which arose in New York, Boston, Philadelphia, and other cities, laid the groundwork for the future Zionist movement in the United States.

These early stirrings of Zionism gained impetus from a number of events that occurred late in the nineteenth century. In 1894, Captain Alfred Dreyfus, a French Jew, was convicted of treason and sentenced to life imprisonment. The captain maintained his innocence and eventually, when the "evidence" against him was exposed as a forgery, he was freed. But the Dreyfus case touched off a wave of anti-Semitism in many parts of Europe, and so became of deep concern to Jews the world over.

The Dreyfus trial inspired Theodor Herzl, an Austrian journalist who was convinced of Dreyfus's innocence, to write a book called *The Jewish State*. In his book, which was published in 1896, Herzl stated his belief that only by establishing a state of their own could the Jewish people solve the problem of anti-Semitism. A year later the first Zionist Congress met in Basel, Switzerland, with Theodor Herzl playing a leading role.

Above, Zionist Theodor Herzl. Below, an early Zionist community.

(56)

Not all in the Jewish community favored the fledgling Zionist movement. Spokesmen for Reform Judaism opposed it on the ground that they had found their Zion in America. Orthodox Jews claimed that only with the coming of the Messiah would Palestine once again become the ancestral homeland of the Jews. Jewish labor leaders were also opposed to Zionism.

In time, opposition to Zionism among leaders of Reform Judaism decreased and the movement gained ground. With the founding of the Zionist Organization of America (ZOA) in 1917, it was well launched in the United States. The outstanding leader of the American Zionist movement was Rabbi Stephen S. Wise. Other prominent leaders were Louis D. Brandeis, Louis Lipsky, Rabbi Hillel Silver, and Henrietta Szold, who, in 1912, founded Hadassah, the largest women's Zionist organization.

The rise of fascism in Germany in the 1930's and the sharp increase of anti-Semitism in Poland and other parts of eastern Europe prior to World War II, created thousands of Jewish refugees. With America closed to them by restrictive immigration laws, many found a haven in Palestine.

Throughout those critical years American Zionists mobilized aid for the struggling Jewish settlements in Palestine. In 1948, when the State of Israel, established by the United Nations, was at war with its neighboring Arab states, the American Jewish community rallied to its support.

Above, Louis D. Brandeis (1856–1941) was famous as a justice of the United States Supreme Court and as a leader of the American Zionist movement. Below, American Zionist leaders Louis Lipsky (left) and Dr. Stephen S. Wise, photographed as they returned from a 1938 world Zionist meeting in London.

Classes for children are often part of the services offered by a synagogue to its community. The photograph (above) shows such a class in the West in 1898. Adults also attended school. Below, a class of the Educational Alliance, where immigrants could learn English.

18

Education and Americanization

Reform Judaism, which German Jewish immigrants had introduced to America in the 1850's, became an established form of religion. But the religion of the eastern European Jews was Orthodox. Some Jews, who wanted to "conserve" many of the old customs, founded yet another form, Conservative Judaism. The Orthodox Jews built their own synagogues and continued to worship as they had for centuries in the Old Country. And whereas the German Jews sent their children to Sunday school for their religious education, the children of the eastern European Jews attended the traditional *cheder* (Hebrew school) they had known in Europe. But there was an important difference. Because the Russian public schools were closed to Jews, the *cheder* in Russia was an all-day school for Jewish children. In America it was an afternoon school because the Jewish immigrants were able to take advantage of the educational opportunities they found in the United States. They saw public education as a stepping stone to a better life. They also built Talmud Torahs and Yeshivas to provide their children with religious instruction. Yeshiva University is an outgrowth of the Yitzhak Elhanan Theological Seminary, which the Russian Jews had founded in 1896.

German Jews were somewhat discomforted by the dress, manners, and language of their eastern European brethren. They wanted the Yiddish-speaking immigrants to become Americanized quickly. That was one of their reasons for founding the Educational Alliance on New York's East Side in 1889. It offered the newcomers a varied educational program for both children and adults. It included courses in English, manual trades, domestic science, and art, as well as a lecture program and a summer camp.

The immigrants benefited from this and similar institutions provided for them by the German Jews. But they also built their own secular culture in the language closest to them—Yiddish. It embraced the press, literature, theater, and later, Yiddish children's schools.

19

Language, Literature, and Theater

The Yiddish press played a vital role in the education and Americanization of the eastern European immigrants. Their newspapers gave them much more than the news of the day. They also contained articles about American history and customs, and short stories and sketches depicting their life in their new homeland — all in the language they understood. It was on the pages of the Yiddish newspapers that the stories of immigrant writers such as Zalmen Libin and Leon Kobrin, and the poems of the labor poets, Morris Rosenfeld, Joseph Bovshover, David Edelstadt, and Morris Winchevski first appeared.

At the turn of the twentieth century other writers gained prominence. Among them were H. Leivik, Moishe Leib Halperin, Mane Leib, Jehoash, Peretz Hirshbein, and Joseph Opatashu, poets and writers whose works the immigrants avidly read in their newspapers before they were published in book form. It could well be said that the Yiddish press laid the foundation for a rich and vibrant American Yiddish literature.

The Yiddish press, with a combined circulation of well over a half a million, reached its peak in 1916. There were five dailies existing at that time. The Socialist-oriented *Jewish Daily Forward*, founded in 1897 and edited by Abraham Cahn, was the largest and most influential among Yiddish-speaking immigrants. Today the *Forward* is still larger than the left-wing *Morning Freiheit*, founded in 1922, the only other remaining daily.

An equally important and even more direct educational role was played by the Yiddish theater. It had many followers among the un-

Above, the editorial office of the Yiddish weekly Di Freie Arbeiter Shtime (The Free Voice of Labor). *Below, a play staged at a Yiddish theater shows life in the Old Country.*

(62)

educated as well as the educated. The most popular presentations were the light musicals and operettas. Although they were frequently of a low artistic level and excessively sentimental and naïve, they held a strong appeal for the immigrants who readily identified with what was presented on the stage — life in the tenements, the sweatshops, the unions, and their first, fumbling efforts at Americanization. The story line of these light entertainments usually included flashbacks to life in the *shtetl*, the little village in the Old Country that the immigrants had left behind them, but to which they were still attached by memories and sentiments. Thus the theater served as an emotional bridge between their past and their present, the Old World and the New.

But there was also a Yiddish theater of a much higher literary level that presented the serious and realistic plays by the immigrant writers Libin and Kobrin; the European playwrights, Abraham Goldfaden, Jacob Gordin, and Sholem Aleichem, who spent the last years of his life in the United States. Later writers, like H. Leivik, I. L. Peretz, Peretz Hirshbein, David Pinski, Sholem Ash, and Osip Dimov saw their plays produced on the stage of the Jewish Art Theater, founded by Maurice Schwartz.

In 1887 there were six full-time Yiddish theater ensembles in New York City alone, plus a number of road companies. In 1928, eleven out of the twenty-four Yiddish theaters around the country were in New York City. Today there is not a single full-time company in New York. Of the two highly regarded nonprofessional Yiddish theater ensembles, *Artef* and *Folksbihne*, the former went out of existence in 1939. The latter performs only periodically.

Above left, writer Sholem Aleichem in 1915, the year before he died. Above right, two outstanding Jewish personalities. Professor Albert Einstein (right), the famous scientist, with actor Maurice Schwartz in costume. Below, "Immortals of the Jewish Stage" — first and second generations of celebrated actresses.

(65)

20

Preserving Liberty in America

Jews in the United States found, over the years, that anti-Jewish prejudice also existed in the New World. Some was a transplant from Europe, brought to America by non-Jewish immigrants; some was home-grown. Although it was never as strong as that which Jews had known in the Old Country, it was, nevertheless, a threat to their liberties. They felt obliged to combat it. In doing so they also defended the liberties of other minorities. The need to guard freedoms at home and abroad led to the formation of a number of defense and relief organizations.

As already mentioned, the oldest of these was B'nai B'rith, founded in 1843. In 1906, the American Jewish Committee, headed by the prominent attorney Louis Marshall, was established. The American Jewish Congress was organized under the leadership of Rabbi Stephen S. Wise in 1917. It was followed, in 1934, by the founding of the Jewish Labor Committee and, in 1936, of the Jewish People's Committee Against Fascism and Anti-Semitism. They were all concerned with the protection of Jewish rights both in the United States and abroad.

The Jewish defense organizations, with the support of many prominent non-Jews, educated the public to the dangers of anti-Semitism. Since racism and anti-Semitism usually go hand-in-hand, Jews often joined with other minorities to fight against a common enemy.

In the twentieth century, as in the nineteenth century, many Jews

Left, the Statue of Liberty in New York Harbor was the symbol of hope to Jews all over the world. Right, this classified advertisement shows just one type of prejudice Jews were up against even in America. Forty out of the forty-seven jobs advertised in this issue of the New York Herald Tribune *specified "Christian."*

THE NEW COLOSSUS.

NOT LIKE THE BRAZEN GIANT OF GREEK FAME,
WITH CONQUERING LIMBS ASTRIDE FROM LAND TO LAND;
HERE AT OUR SEA-WASHED, SUNSET GATES SHALL STAND
A MIGHTY WOMAN WITH A TORCH, WHOSE FLAME
IS THE IMPRISONED LIGHTNING, AND HER NAME
MOTHER OF EXILES, FROM HER BEACON-HAND
GLOWS WORLD-WIDE WELCOME; HER MILD EYES COMMAND
THE AIR-BRIDGED HARBOR THAT TWIN CITIES FRAME.
"KEEP ANCIENT LANDS, YOUR STORIED POMP!"
        CRIES SHE
WITH SILENT LIPS. "GIVE ME YOUR TIRED, YOUR
        POOR,
YOUR HUDDLED MASSES YEARNING TO BREATHE FREE,
THE WRETCHED REFUSE OF YOUR TEEMING SHORE.
SEND THESE, THE HOMELESS, TEMPEST-TOST TO ME,
I LIFT MY LAMP BESIDE THE GOLDEN DOOR!"

———

THIS TABLET, WITH HER SONNET TO THE BARTHOLDI STATUE
OF LIBERTY ENGRAVED UPON IT, IS PLACED UPON THESE WALLS
IN LOVING MEMORY OF

EMMA LAZARUS

BORN IN NEW YORK CITY, JULY 22D. 1849
DIED NOVEMBER 19TH. 1887.

joined black people in their struggle for civil rights. Jews were among the founders of the National Association for the Advancement of Colored People (NAACP) in 1909. And the Spingarn brothers, Joel Elias and Arthur B., held national offices in the organization for many years. A large number of Jews, like Andrew Goodman and Michael Schwerner, were active in the civil-rights movement of the 1960's, some giving their labor; others, their money; and some, their lives. Their role in this movement, however, has declined as black people have sought to increase their control over their own lives and their own fate in America.

"The New Colossus," the sonnet that appears on the base of the Statue of Liberty and that welcomes immigrants to America's shores, was written by Emma Lazarus (1849–1887), a Jewish-American poet and essayist.

(69)

21

The New Deal and Anti-Semitism

During the 1930's, the economic crisis at home and the rise of fascism abroad led to a sharp increase in American anti-Semitism. The masses of unemployed became fertile ground for native hate groups who saw in the Jew a convenient scapegoat to blame for the depression.

The largest and most influential of these hate-groups was the Christian Front led by a Detroit priest, Father Charles E. Coughlin. His weekly anti-Semitic radio broadcasts reached millions of listeners, and his newspaper, *Social Justice*, was sold on the streets of many cities.

As Hitler was preparing to launch World War II, he poured millions of dollars into these hate-mongering organizations enabling them to step up their anti-Semitic and pro-Nazi propaganda in order to divide and thus weaken the country.

President Roosevelt took a number of measures to put the country back on its feet, and this was called the "New Deal."

Among the presidential advisers who helped plan and shape the New Deal program were justice of the Supreme Court Felix Frankfurter and union leaders Sidney Hillman and David Dubinsky. Anti-Semitic enemies of the president attacked the "Jew Deal" and "President Rosenfelt."

When the United States united to fight World War II, bigots found it more and more difficult to peddle their racial prejudices. Both the war needs and legislation enacted under the New Deal, dealt hard blows to discriminatory practices in labor, housing, and education.

Above, in the depression years of the 1930's anyone who got a job worked — even children. Below, Father Charles Coughlin, a Detroit priest, broadcast weekly anti-Semitic programs to millions of Americans. Father Coughlin blamed the Jews for America's problems.

(70)

But the war only limited the activities of the reactionaries and anti-Semites. It did not silence them completely. One of their favorite targets was Sidney Hillman, who held such key wartime positions in Washington as Associate Director of the Office of Production Management and Director of the Labor Division of the War Production Board. Addressing a union convenion in 1944, at the height of the war, Hillman found it necessary to say, "Yes, and Jew-baiting — you may as well put that right on top; it is here. There are lots of people who don't want to discuss bigotry, but I would rather have it in the open than to have it under cover. It is not surprising . . . that the native American fascists have been screaming about the "Jew Deal," . . . . and that [they] drag in the fact that I am a Jew and that I was born in Lithuania. And I don't apologize to anybody for it."

At the end of the war, when it was discovered that the Nazis had killed 6 million Jews, a third of the world's Jewish population, the American public reacted with a sense of revulsion to anti-Semitism. There was also a feeling of sympathy for surviving Jews. An expression of that sympathy was the support the American people gave for the establishment of the State of Israel.

22

Today's Problems and Trends

Jews today are acutely aware of how far they have come in American life. Yet they are also convinced they still have a way to go to defeat anti-Semitism. A recent survey by the Anti-Defamation League revealed that "anti-Semitism is widespread and pervasive" among almost a third of Americans. There are still many places Jews cannot reach as easily as other Americans, despite laws against discrimination.

In the days of mass immigration it was thought that America would become a "melting pot" of nationalities, that the price of Americanization would be the loss of national identity. Time has proved this theory wrong. Today, American Jews are more acutely aware of their Jewish identity than ever before. And consciousness of identity leads to a quest for heritage, for a deeper understanding of one's history and culture. The growing trend in universities to introduce Jewish studies programs in the curriculum is a reflection of that quest.

Many young Jews are finding in their heritage a guide to changing social values and a responsible involvement in the moral issues of our times. They look upon it as an inspiration in their struggle for peace, justice, and equality.

Though individual Jews may be divided on such questions as intermarriage, religious affiliation, and the meaning of Jewishness, the Jewish community as a whole is united on the basic issues related to Jewish survival. The two events in recent history that forged this unity are the Nazi slaughter of six million European Jews and the establishment of the State of Israel. The first sharpened the Jews' awareness of the dangers of anti-Semitism and the need to combat it wherever it manifests itself. The second gave them a feeling of national pride that Jews have not known in over two thousand years.

As a minority, American Jews can never achieve full equality, or secure the rights they have won, so long as other minorities are still dis-

In 1972, Sally J. Priesand became the first woman rabbi in the history of Judaism: a new direction for an old religion.

criminated against. The struggle for full equality — civil, political, economic — is a common struggle of all minorities.

In maintaining their national and cultural identity, American Jews, like all other ethnic groups, are strengthening and enriching the national and cultural life of America as a whole. "The symphony of America," wrote Rabbi Judah L. Magnes, "must be written by the various nationalities which keep their individual and characteristic note, and which sound this note in harmony with their sister nationalities." In this symphony of nationalities American Jews sound their own unique note.

Some Twentieth-Century
Jews Who Contributed
to American Life

BERNARD MANNES BARUCH	Financier — Presidential Adviser
SAUL BELLOW	Author
IRVING BERLIN	Songwriter
LEONARD BERNSTEIN	Composer — Conductor
FANNY BRICE	Actress
BENJAMIN CARDOZO	Jurist — Supreme Court Justice
JO DAVIDSON	Sculptor
BOB DYLAN	Folk Singer — Composer
ALBERT EINSTEIN	Physicist — Nobel Prize Winner
MISCHA ELMAN	Musician — Concert Violinist
JACOB EPSTEIN	Sculptor
EDNA FERBER	Author
FELIX FRANKFURTER	Jurist — Supreme Court Justice
GEORGE GERSHWIN	Composer
MICHAEL GOLD	Author
ARTHUR J. GOLDBERG	Jurist — Supreme Court Justice — U.S. Ambassador to the United Nations
HANK GREENBERG	Baseball Player
LILLIAN HELLMAN	Playwright
VLADIMIR HOROWITZ	Musician — Concert Pianist
GEORGE S. KAUFMAN	Playwright
DANNY KAYE	Actor
SANDY KOUFAX	Baseball Player
HERBERT H. LEHMAN	Senator — New York Governor
BENNY LEONARD	Prizefighter
NORMAN MAILER	Author
BERNARD MALAMUD	Author

MARX BROTHERS	Actors
YEHUDI MENUHIN	Musician — Concert Violinist
ARTHUR MILLER	Playwright
HENRY MORGENTHAU, JR.	Cabinet Member — Secretary of the Treasury
PAUL MUNI	Actor
ADOLPH SIMON OCHS	Publisher — Founder of *The New York Times*
CLIFFORD ODETS	Playwright
SAMUEL ORNITZ	Author
ISADOR I. RABI	Physicist — Nobel Prize Winner
ABRAHAM A. RIBICOFF	Governor of Connecticut — Cabinet Member — Senator
JULIUS ROSENWALD	Business Leader — Founder of Sears Roebuck & Company
HENRY ROTH	Author
PHILIP ROTH	Author
JONAS E. SALK	Bacteriologist — developed anti-polio vaccine
JACOB HENRY SCHIFF	Banker — Philanthropist
BEN SHAHN	Painter
ALFRED STIEGLITZ	Photographer
HAROLD C. UREY	Chemist — Nobel Prize Winner
SELMAN A. WAKSMAN	Microbiologist — Nobel Prize Winner
ABRAHAM WALKOWITZ	Painter
FELIX MORITZ WARBURG	Banker — Philanthropist
WARNER BROTHERS	Producers
MAX WEBER	Painter

Left, Bernard Mannes Baruch (1870–1965) served as an adviser to several American presidents. He wrote a number of books and worked to control atomic weapons. Right, Leonard Bernstein (1918–   ) is best known for his years as conductor of the New York Philharmonic Orchestra. In addition, he has composed music, appeared on television as a performer and teacher, and taken part in American social and political issues.

Fanny Brice (1891–1951) was a brilliant comedienne of stage, screen, and radio. The play and film Funny Girl, starring Barbra Streisand, were based on her life.

Above, award-winning sculptor Jo Davidson (1883–1952) with one of his famous subjects, writer Gertrude Stein (1874–1946), whose home in France attracted the outstanding writers and artists of her day. This photograph shows the sculptor, the artist, and the statue. Above right, folksinger and composer Bob Dylan (1941–   ) became a hero in his time, known for such songs as "Blowin' in the Wind" and for the advent of folk-rock in twentieth-century music. Below right, Edna Ferber (1887–   ) has written novels, short stories, and plays. In addition to the Pulitzer prize-winning So Big, *her novels include* Show Boat, Cimarron, Saratoga Trunk, *and* Giant.

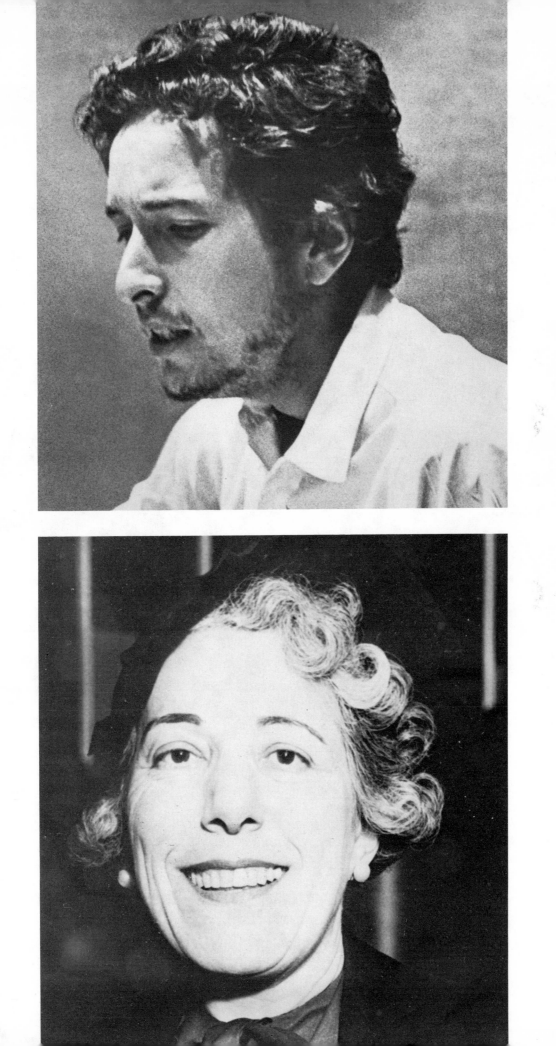

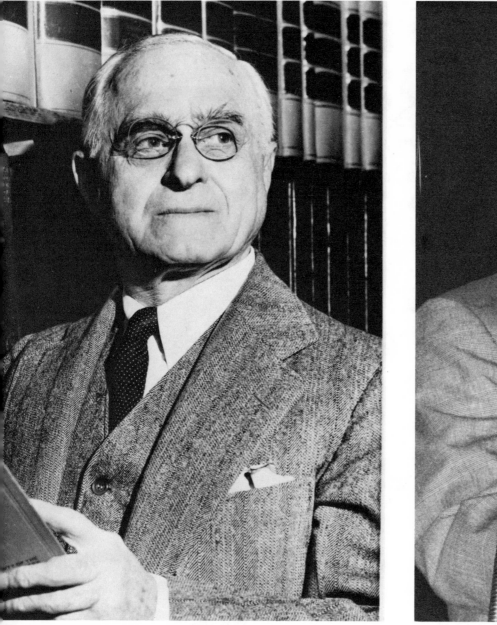

Above left, jurist and writer Felix Frankfurter (1882–1965) served as a justice of the United States Supreme Court. Above right, Arthur J. Goldberg (1908–   ), shown at a commemorative service of the Warsaw ghetto uprising against the Nazis during World War II, has served the United States as secretary of labor, Supreme Court justice, and ambassador to the United Nations. Right, Lillian Hellman (1905–   ) is known primarily for her plays, which include The Children's Hour *and* The Little Foxes.

(82)

Above, actress and singing star Barbra Streisand (1942–   ), with Canadian Prime Minister Trudeau in 1970. The Marx Brothers (above right) rank high among America's outstanding comedy personalities. They are, left to right, Zeppo, Harpo, Chico, and Groucho. Their film credits include A Night at the Opera *and* A Day at the Races. *Sandy Koufax (1935–   ) was a record-breaking left-handed pitcher for several years with the Los Angeles Dodgers. Koufax left baseball because of his health and now works occasionally as a sports commentator. He attracted attention because he would not play ball on the High Holy Days. In 1972 he was elected to the Baseball Hall of Fame.*

Above, Connecticut lawyer Abraham A. Ribicoff (1910–) entered national politics under President John F. Kennedy. Ribicoff has served as governor of his state, secretary of health, education, and welfare under Kennedy, and as a United States senator. With the development of an anti-polio vaccine, Jonas E. Salk (1914–) helped virtually to eliminate that crippling disease.

(86)

Index

Yuri Suhl came to the United States as a young immigrant from Poland. He attended City College in Brooklyn and New York University. Mr. Suhl has written several volumes of Yiddish poetry and a number of books in English. Among the latter are: *One Foot in America* (a novel); *They Fought Back* (the factual account of Jewish resistance to Nazi slaughter); a biography of Ernestine Rose; and *Simon Boom Gives a Wedding* (his first book for children). At present Mr. Suhl divides his time between writing, teaching, and sculpting with found objects. He and his wife live in New York City.

William Loren Katz has long been involved in uncovering long-buried facts about the roles of minority groups in American history. For fifteen years he taught United States history at the secondary level. He has also served as a consultant to state departments of education and to the Smithsonian Institution. His credits as a writer include the award-winning *Eyewitness: The Negro in American History* (1967), *American Majorities and Minorities* (1970), and *The Black West: A Documentary and Pictorial History* (1971). Currently Mr. Katz is a scholar-in-residence at Teachers College, Columbia University.